MEAN *girls*
all grown up

workbook & journal

a spiritual guide
to surviving mean women

Hayley DiMarco

pinkm⊕sphere
a part of Hungry Planet

R
Revell
Grand Rapids, Michigan

Published by Fleming H. Revell
a division of Baker Publishing Group
P.O. Box 6287, Grand Rapids, MI 49516-6287

Printed in the United States of America

ISBN 0-8007-3106-9

Published in association with Yates & Yates, LLP, Literary Agents, Orange, California.

contents

mean diagnosis

freeing your soul from the bondage of mean

healing from the inside out

finding inner peace in the face of mean

living with the memory of mean

the end of the journey

It is impossible
to enter into communion
with God
when you are in a
critical temper;
it makes you hard
and vindictive and cruel,
and leaves you
with the flattering unction
that you are a superior person.

—Oswald Chambers

mean diagnosis

what it's all about

Mean Girls are everywhere. If you look hard enough you'll find one under every rock. And they are there at every age. From high school to middle age, they never seem to give up. In *Mean Girls All Grown Up*, I talked a lot about how to handle the Mean Girl in your life. But in this workbook and journal we are going to take a closer look inside you. We are going to take a journey of the spirit.

What really matters in this world isn't what other people are doing, saying, or thinking. The only thing that really matters from the perspective of eternity is your spirit and what you allow it to become. The ancient wisdom goes that you should only work to change the things that you have the power to change. Any attempt to change things out of your control is an exercise in futility.

When it comes to getting rid of the mean in your life, two basic forces are at work: yourself and the other woman. Knowing that you have no power over her but a great deal of power over yourself, it stands to reason that the bulk of your effort should be in that direction—inward. And so the *Mean Girls All Grown Up Workbook and Journal* is a tool just for you. In this small book you won't find the same things you did in *Mean Girls All Grown Up*. You won't find a list of ways to react to her or things to say to her. This isn't a line-by-line guide to managing the Mean Girl; instead, it's a trip through the inner workings of your heart and soul. The journal pages are there to help you delve deep into your heart and see what lies hidden that might be adding to the emotional turmoil of living with mean. Use them as an exercise in spiritual honesty. Risk making a change that will impact your mind and emotions.

What I hope you find in the pages of this book is truth—the truth that will shine the light of eternity on your spirit and give you wings to rise above the mundane and morbid aspects of life with a Mean Girl nipping at your heels. Read this book however you desire. From front to back, back to front, or somewhere in between. Read it daily, nightly, weekly, whatever your soul desires, but read it carefully and test it. See if the truth contained inside these pages doesn't lift your spirit and help you to see things from a more divine perspective. This book can be done solo or with a close friend. Either way, risk honesty. Dare to dive deep inside yourself and discover the part of your soul that yearns for peace with the divine.

Do You Have a Mean Girl Problem?

If you aren't sure whether this book is for you or not, give this a try. Take the following quiz and see if you have a Mean Girl problem that needs some spiritual salve.

Answer the following:

Do you have a mean woman in your life?   Yes   No

Have you lost a man to another woman?   Yes   No

Do you have mainly male friends?   Yes   No

Have you been mad at another woman in the past two weeks?
    Yes   No

Have you ever had to teach a woman a lesson?   Yes   No

Do you do all you can to avoid women because they're just plain
    mean?   Yes   No

If you answered yes to two or more of these, then you probably have a Mean Girl problem. This guide is designed to help you understand God's will for you when it comes to women who seem bent on destroying you. He has something important to say to you about her and, more importantly, about you. My hope is that his will won't be such a mystery any longer after you take a walk through this workbook and journal.

Selah. Stop. Breathe. Think.

This book starts with you and it ends with you. That's why I want you to start with some journaling right off the bat. (Later on, some of the journal pages will just be blank for you to write down any thoughts you need to. But this time I'm going to give you a few questions to help you get started.) Before we delve into the truth about mean, let's take some time to do a spiritual inventory of ourselves. It will do us good to think about what our soul is crying out for and what we hope to find within ourselves as we take this journey. So open up your heart as we look into the inner workings of your soul.

What is missing from your spiritual life right now?

Describe the spiritual life that you'd like to have.

Selah

Are you willing to experience a change in your heart and mind in order to relieve the pain of mean? What's more, are you willing to work to free your spirit from the Mean Girl's bondage?

What three things will you commit to do in the next week that will draw you closer in your relationship with God (journaling, meditation, prayer, reading, etc.)?

What three things bother you most about your Mean Girl problems?

How would you like to act around mean women in the future? Are there ways you have acted in the past that you wish you could erase?

What is your goal when it comes to your Mean Girl problems?

Selah

What do you want from this book? Why did you pick it up? What aspect of your life do you want to be changed after reading this book?

List two women you will pray for while you are reading this book:

If you have a friend or two who might benefit from taking this same journey, list them below. Then talk to them about doing this study with you. Being vulnerable and reading your journaling thoughts together will help you both to dig deeper into your souls and clean out the muddy parts.

freeing your soul from the bondage of mean

What other women think of you
cannot determine your success

What other women think of you cannot determine your success—or you would be a failure in all that you do. There is no way in the world everyone will like you or what you do. You can't let that bother you. Even if a mean woman considers your vision a distraction and your calling in life a big mistake, she can't be your gauge for fulfillment or happiness. Only *you* truly know what God has called you to do. Only *you* know the purpose that God has assigned your life. How faithful would you be if you let everyone's opinion of your vision change that very vision? Remember this: if your calling isn't tested, you will never know if it is truly a calling. For just as the refiner's fire burns away the dross from the gold, so your testing will separate the fake calling from the true. Instead of fearing the test on your calling, then, look for it. If it isn't there, then the vision itself is probably not from God. For anything he calls us to do must be tested to be proven right and good.

dive

1. Think about the dreams you have. Which of them have been the hardest to attain? Can you understand how a real dream has to be tested to prove itself? Think about *American Idol*. Each contestant's dream of being a star has to be tested every week with difficult music performed live in front of millions of people. But the ones who stand the test get the prize and see their dreams unfold in front of their eyes. What dream do you have that you are willing to have tested to prove it is good? Do you have a dream that you just don't want to fight for? Then maybe that isn't a dream after all. Remember, *"The refining pot is for silver and the furnace for gold, but the LORD tests hearts"* (Proverbs 17:3 NASB).

2. Think about the Mean Girl in your life. How does she try to kill your dreams? Imagine her as a tool for your refining. The next time she does something to cut you down, think about it as another part of the proving ground, proving that you will not give up on who you are, who you dream to be, or the holiness you wish to attain.

3. Write out your dreams on the journal pages. Write down the things you are willing to go to the mat for. And then when the testing comes, thank God that he wants to help you be strong enough to live your dream.

Selah

stop   breathe   think

Controlling what others think about you is a giant waste of time

The hardest thing in the world to overcome is thinking we have to control what others think about us. All our efforts are wrapped up in what other people think of us. Are we kind enough, smart enough, cute enough, faithful enough? Do they think us wise, bright, honorable? Are we rich enough, successful enough? We spend all our energy trying to look better to the rest of the world. But all of this is a waste of our time because what others think is not our responsibility. Nor is it even within our power. The urge to justify and to position ourselves must be fought, for it is Christ who justifies and God who defends. To do so yourself is to take away God's very own role. He'll justify. He'll take care of you. Trust the Creator and peace will be yours.

dive

1. Do you have a good or a bad self-image? Whatever you answered, realize that it doesn't matter, because a woman who understands that it isn't what *others* think about her or even what *she* thinks about herself but only what *God* thinks that ultimately matters is so led by her spirit that she is free to fail, free to make mistakes, and free to not fit in. When you ultimately understand whose opinion *really* matters, you blossom, and the world will begin to notice. Today change your concerns about yourself into concerns about your spirit. Where does its energy go? What does it focus on? If you can't find beauty around you, then look harder. God has placed it everywhere. Today find beauty outside yourself and thank God each time you do.

2. How have you tried to justify yourself in the past week? Did it work? Think about who you were trying to convince. Tell God today that you trust him to straighten others out and that you will no longer be concerned with winning. What is more important to you, being peaceful or being right?

3. "*Many are the plans in the mind of a man, but it is the purpose of the Lord that will stand*" (Proverbs 19:21 ESV). You can plan and manipulate your life and others' lives all you want, but in the end who do you think prevails? Whatever you plan or devise in your mind, run it by the all-knowing mind of God. Does it please him? If not, beware.

Selah

A person without self-control
is as defenseless as a city
with broken-down walls.

—King Solomon in the book of Proverbs,
chapter 25, verse 28 NLT

stop   breathe   think

Don't judge others
for their shortcomings

If the only thing you have control of is yourself, then complaining about the shortcomings of others is not only sinful but destructive. Constantly being occupied with things beyond your control leaves you feeling frustrated and bitter. The sins of others become more and more obvious the closer you draw to God—but so do your own sins, so concentrate on those and leave others' improvement to them. Stop wrestling with thoughts of how bad they are and confess that just by thinking such a thing you show yourself to be worse than them.

dive

1. Complaining is so very unattractive. No one likes to be around someone who finds fault with everything. Think about your world. Is it ugly, bitter, and resentful, or is it positive, hopeful, and energetic? If you are feeling worn out by the world, then stop complaining. The next time you get ready to complain, stop yourself and say something nice, something positive. Today is the day. Turn over a new leaf. Become Ms. Positive and your spirit will soar.

2. You know that the only thing you have control of is yourself, so why not exercise a bit of self-control? Show your body and your mind who is in charge. Determine that you will change something today—an old habit, complaining, whining, an overeating problem, an under-eating problem. He has given you the power; only your trust of that power is lacking. *"For God did not give us a spirit of timidity, but a spirit of power, of love and of self-discipline"* (2 Timothy 1:7). Change something about you that you thought you could never change, because what you can't change controls you. Remember, some say it takes 29 days to make a new habit, so buck up and take control of your body, your life, and your spirit. Don't give up and don't give in.

It is estimated that over their forty years of wandering, God allowed over one million of the children of Israel to die in the wilderness **because of their complaining.**

—Bowes, quoted in
The Encyclopedia of 7700 Illustrations

Selah

stop   breathe   think

At the **moment** you blame, you lose control

We can make our plans, but the Lord determines our steps.

—the book of Proverbs*

When you blame others for what happens to you, you waste your energy and destroy your faith. Since it isn't what happens to you but what you *think* about what happens to you that matters, no one has the power to control your life. So blaming others for what happens to you is a futile matter that only dilutes the power of self-control that God wants you to maintain. We can have no self-control as long as we are giving all the control over to others who either attempt to or unintentionally manipulate us.

Truly healthy people find no need to blame either themselves or others for their misfortunes. God determines the steps of man, not the man, nor his friends, nor his enemies. How long will you allow a world that has no real power to have power over you?

Things happen. Don't allow things to be that which control you, for a man is a slave to whatever has mastered him (2 Peter 2:19). To be a slave to anyone or anything less than God is complete disobedience to the first commandment—"have no other gods before me" (Exodus 20:3). Determine to set your thoughts on what is good, and choose not to blame others for the steps the Lord has laid for you.

* Proverbs 16:9 NLT

dive

1. Who have you given control of your life to? The best way to figure this out is to determine who you think about the most. Whoever occupies most of your thought time is the one in control of your life.

2. Who do you blame? Are there people in your life that you blame for how things are? This is a position of weakness. You are giving control over to others when you think like this. No one can control your spirit or your mind but you, and in the end that's all that matters. A mind free to think on things of peace, hope, and light is a mind under control of no one but God. Today confess to God that you blame others. List them, then set them free of blame. Decide that you and your God alone are in control of your destiny.

3. What do you have faith in? Is God big enough to carry your world? Or have you created a backup for him? Think about who runs your world.

4. Read the Ten Commandments today. Get a Bible and find Exodus 20. Meditate on the age-old truth found there. Do you believe it? Do you live it?

Selah

Have you noticed? When she gossips,
she's a backstabbing vixen,
but when you gossip, you're just
sharing with your friend.

stop   breathe   think

Don't take *rejection* as insight on the will of God

In our attempt to seek the will of God that we so long for, we often take any sign we see as the sign that God wants us to give up. But in fact, the opposite might be true. God must test your faith for it to be proven and refined. Your calling must be tested. If there isn't a battle to fight, then you must be doing something wrong. Progress requires resistance.

Check your vision. If there isn't someone trying to stop or dissuade you, then it's probably not the battle you need to be fighting.

dive

1. Everybody has a dream, although they might be afraid to admit it. What is your dream? Have you told anyone? Have you considered if it is an honorable dream? One that you can be proud of? If so, then watch for opposition. When you see it, simply smile and thank God that he finds you worthy of testing. Prove your dream good by sticking to it even in the face of opposition. Ancient wisdom passed down through generations says, *"The crucible for silver and the furnace for gold, but the* LORD *tests the heart"* (Proverbs 17:3).

2. Check your opposition. Listen to what the Mean Girls say, consider it, and if there is a shred of truth or good advice in what they say, take it to heart. Practice harder, work longer, do whatever it takes to achieve that dream you have been entrusted with. This week write down two things that you will work on to bring you closer to your dream.

Selah

stop   breathe   think.

No one can insult you

Women might try to insult you. They might accuse you or even abuse you. But it isn't the women themselves who hurt you. Rather it is how you think about the insult that determines if you will be hurt or not. You can choose to ignore the statement or even to consider where she is coming from. But she can't hurt you unless you choose to take it that way. For it is never the thing itself but how you choose to think about the thing that hurts.

A rebuke impresses
a man of discernment more than
a hundred lashes a fool.
—Proverbs 17:10

dive

1. Today write about a woman who insulted you or cut you down—but write about the incident from her perspective. Try to imagine what she was feeling that would make her do what she did.

2. Consider how you can think about what she said or did in a different way. What she said can't physically hurt you, so it's what you are thinking that hurts. Write down three things about this event that you could use for your good. Try to find something positive to focus on instead of the bad part.

Selah

stop   breathe   think.

Friends are essential for a healthy spiritual life

Community is the key to managing your spiritual life and your Mean Girl problem. Without a concerted effort to make and keep friends, you become more and more a victim to the whims of the Mean Girl and the deterioration of your spirit. You must develop healthy relationships that feed your spirit and nurture your emotions. It is through the trials and joys of friendship that we learn to sail on rough waters and keep the boat afloat. If you demand perfection from someone before they can be your friend, you will forever be friendless. Allow people to be human, forgive them, love them, and protect them as they will protect you from the slings and arrows of the Mean Girl.

dive

1. How many good friends do you have? If you can't really claim any, then make a plan for who you will pursue. Begin to be nice to them. Ask them to do things. Care about them. Find at least two good friends you can look to for support and companionship. If you already have friends, then make sure you are taking care of them. There is power in numbers, so don't let yourself become a lone wolf, or you'll be an easy target for the Mean Girl.

Selah

Have you noticed?
When she nags people
about their flaws, she is being
critical and witchy, but when
you do, you're just being helpful.

healing from the inside out

Fruit is grown in the **trials** of life

Every difficult situation in life offers us the opportunity to access the strength of our spirit. Instead of fearing these painful situations, we should look at them as a time for strengthening. For a muscle unused becomes weak, but a muscle that is often used is refined, lean, and powerful. In order to become fully manifest in your spirit, the fruit of the spirit must be exercised, and it is in these fiery trials that they get the opportunity to work. Are you being treated badly? Call upon the gift of patience. Are you tempted by a desire within your reach but beyond righteousness? Then call upon self-control. Use these trials as opportunities to grow your fruit into the powerful tools that were designed for you.

dive

Here is a list of fruit of the Spirit—tools that strengthen you and bring you to a place of healing and wholeness. Some might seem hard to live out, even bad for you, but for a healthy spirit they are crucial. Read Galatians 5:22–23.

love	goodness
joy	faithfulness
peace	gentleness
patience	self-control
kindness	

Go over the list and see which come to you naturally. Then look at those that don't come so easily. How will you discipline yourself to attain them? Spiritual discipline is necessary for growing spiritual fruit. I recommend reading one of the best books on spiritual discipline, *Celebration of Discipline* by Richard Foster.

If suffering is completely in God's hands, why don't we just leave it up to His will? Why don't we believe that, just as He can bring us back to a trial when we run away, He can also protect us when we don't run away?

—Tertullian

Selah

stop   breathe   think

What you have lost has merely been **returned** to where it came from

Do not worry about losing what you *think*
you own, because in the truest sense of the word
you don't *own* anything. Everything belongs to God to
do with as he sees fit. Nothing owned by Job belonged to
Job (read his story in the Bible's book of Job), and nothing
belongs to you. So instead of feeling angry or hurt because
of what has been taken from you, just tell yourself that it
has been returned to God to care for and redistribute or
protect. Don't be angry with the woman who has taken
it from you. It's not your job to decide who God uses
for what purpose. Instead, be like a traveler who
rents a car and cares for it while traveling but
returns it to the owner as she goes on her
way.

dive

Let go. If someone you think is yours has been turned against you or taken from you, rethink your position. Spend some time in prayer allowing God to take back what is really his. Try this: Close your eyes, imagine the person, and imagine walking up to God and leading this person into his arms. Then imagine turning and walking away, trusting God to do what he wants with the person.

Selah

stop   breathe   think

Avoid the cares and anxieties of this world

Avoid the cares and anxieties of this world, because they are just momentary distractions from your real purpose. To allow them to consume you is to take your focus off your goal, the prize for which you were made. Beware of returning to what you renounced. Before you took on the Spirit of the Lord you managed your world with all of your energy, and now you have to resist the urge to go back into that same state of mind. If you did, you would be like the man who was carrying a heavy load when he was picked up by a kind farmer in a cart. The farmer offered him a ride and helped him on board, but as they rode on, the man with the load continued to labor to keep it on his shoulders. "Why do you not let down your load since I have picked you up?" asked the farmer. "Oh, it was so nice of you to pick me up," said the man with the load. "I couldn't burden you further with letting down my load." Don't be like that man. Trust the divine power of God and allow your burden to be lifted.

dive

1. What are you carrying that is weighing you down? If you are living for your divine purpose, then you should feel light and airy, not heavy and burdened. Meditate on this truth, the words of the Christ who said, *"Come to Me, all who are weary and heavy-laden, and I will give you rest. Take My yoke upon you and learn from Me, for I am gentle and humble in heart, and <u>you will find rest for your souls</u>. For My yoke is easy and <u>My burden is light</u>"* (Matthew 11:28–30 NASB). Will you be like the man in the wagon who still carried his load though the wagon was underneath him?

2. Make a list of the things you will let go of today. Focus on your purpose and your holiness and let the other things fall through the cracks, trusting God to pick them up. After you write the list, take it to a fireplace or some other place safe for burning and burn it, representing to yourself and to God that you will let go of controlling the things that only make you anxious because you can't control them.

Selah

stop   breathe   think

If people aren't better for having known you, then you aren't *loving* them

But I say to you, Love your enemies and pray for those who persecute you.

—Jesus Christ, Matthew 5:44 ESV

Those who are holy understand that life isn't about them; it's about loving and serving the world, including the Mean Girls of the world. If you have a woman who is mean to you, then the holy thing to do is to care for her. What an honor and what a responsibility to be the mature one who knows that life is more than catfights and fitting in. Life is about being true to yourself and honoring God by honoring his creation, even the mean parts. The winning soul is the one who is secure enough in her position in God's heart to know that persecution only makes her stronger, not weaker, and that fighting to be heard is weakness, not power. Confidence means having the strength to laugh in the face of insults and to know that in the grand scheme of things they mean nothing.

dive

1. Think about these words spoken by Jesus Christ: *Love your enemies*. Do you have the strength of spirit to do that? If not you, then who? He was talking to all of us, not just priests and nuns. Everyone who truly loves, loves those who hate them, for it's not real love to love only those who love you back. How will you love your enemy? What will you do this week that is loving? Turn the other cheek? Not retaliate? Not gossip? Not hate? What will you do to love?

2. Prayer works. Use it. Pray that her spirit would be lightened and that her anger would subside. Pray for her every day this week—not for yourself, but for her good.

Selah

stop   breathe   think

You don't have to feel good
to have peace

Men sometimes think women are crazy because we feel things so deeply, but the truth is, we aren't crazy because of what we feel but because of how we act on our feelings. Feelings are healthy to some extent. They help us understand our wants and sometimes our needs. But the trouble comes when we think something is terribly wrong if we don't feel good all the time. The truth is, it's normal to just feel awful sometimes. Feeling depressed doesn't always mean the end of the world. Sometimes it's just a season. It's just a hormone. It's just an empty stomach or mind. Don't lie to yourself and believe that you *have* to feel good all the time to be normal. Every woman in the world feels crappy sometimes. The thing to remember is that feelings aren't reality, and they don't always have to be analyzed ("What's wrong with me?") or obeyed ("I'm feeling depressed so I won't go to work today"). Sometimes the brain has to take over and deny the emotion any territory. It may still be there, but you don't have to listen to it like the gospel. Especially when it comes to hormones—sometimes they just mess with you and get you feeling all kinds of weird things. Just do what I do: tell yourself, "This will pass." I find that when I remember that everything is temporary when it comes to feelings, I am much happier. The worst thing to do is to think it will never change—to think, "I'll always feel awful!" It isn't true, so don't buy the lie.

dive

Write about your awful feelings. Describe them like a good journalist. Look at them objectively and write about the truth. Remember when you felt good and the last time you felt bad. Then remember when that ended. Do what you can to convince yourself that feelings can't run your life.

Selah

stop   breathe   think

If a habit is bad,
don't feed it

Habits are the creation of repeated action. They grow or de-
crease based on repetition. If you habitually read, you will
become a better reader. If you regularly exercise, you will
become stronger. It is the same with your spirit. When-
ever you are envious, you strengthen your envy. You
nurture it and grow its power in your life.

If you don't want to live with envy, then don't
continue to feed it every time it pops up. Give
it nothing to support its life. If you will for-
sake it and strive to end the repetition
of envy—even if you succeed only
every other time—it will slowly
get better. Soon you'll achieve
a day of avoiding it, then a
week of avoiding it, and
eventually the harm-
ful emotion will
be replaced by
a healthier
one.

dive

If envy isn't your sin of choice, then what is? Think of something that plagues you and makes you feel miserable—like anger, resentment, loneliness, jealousy—then stop feeding it. Turn it off at every chance. Change the channel, go on to another subject, get out of the environment that is causing it. Each time you do this, you will weaken its grip on you.

Things appear difficult to us only when
we don't remember God.

—Chrysostom

Selah

stop   breathe   think

Other women
are *essential* to life

How do you feel about women? Do you trust them? Are they generally nice? Think about your feelings toward women in general. When you walk into a room and you see two tables, one with mainly women and one with mainly men, which table do you go to? Why?

Other women are essential to your life. You might think that right now men "get you," but the only one who will ever truly "get you" is another woman. Men can never completely understand how you feel, no matter how much they say they do. They don't feel the way we do. They don't have the same hormones coursing through their veins; they don't have the same things in life happening to them. They'll never have cramps or a baby. They're just different—good, but different.

Every woman should have at least one good girlfriend she can trust. One she can stay up talking to till four in the morning. One she can call when she's crying or when she's sick. If you'd like to have more girlfriends in your life and fewer Mean Girls, then think about how you feel about women. If you don't trust them, they'll never trust you. Sometimes you have to risk being hurt in order to find friendship.

dive

Today write about how you feel about women. What you feel when you see them walking down the hall or in the mall. How they make you feel when they talk, when you laugh together, when they scratch your back. Write about the good in women and the bad in women. How can you start to accept the bad so you can get to the good?

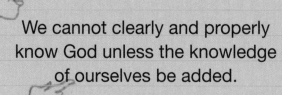

We cannot clearly and properly
know God unless the knowledge
of ourselves be added.

—John Calvin

Selah

stop   breathe   think

finding *inner peace* in the face of mean

Don't allow *affection* to become your **affliction**

One is afflicted by affection when one becomes addicted to the need for it. Affection from others cannot be the object of your attention. It shouldn't concern you if other women like you or not. If you are acting in accord with your faith, you can't become preoccupied with what *she* thinks of you. Once you are determined that everyone has to like you, you are controlled by that desire more than by your God. You become a victim of your need for affection. The truly spiritual woman is so concerned with pleasing God that she can't become preoccupied with human inattention. And her mantra becomes, "Seek first the kingdom of God and his righteousness, and all these things will be added to you" (Matthew 6:33 ESV).

dive

1. Addiction is having a compulsive need for something. What are you addicted to? What things in your life today do you feel that you just must have? Do you have to have people liking you? How do you feel when a woman doesn't like you? Is your feeling healthy, or can you choose to change the way you think and reduce your addiction?

2. A person concerned about pleasing God has little time to worry about pleasing people. Would you like freedom from the stress of pleasing people and the need to be needed or feel loved? Find out what pleases God and go after that with all your energy this week. When it comes to your Mean Girl, pick up *Mean Girls All Grown Up* and find out what God requires of you.

3. This week try being more concerned with helping other women than with helping yourself to feel good. Each time you feel left out, alone, or hurt, turn that off and tell yourself, *Not myself but serving others, that is my goal this week*. You will soon find that a woman who isn't focused on herself is a happier woman.

Selah

Have you noticed?
When she doesn't like your friends,
she's being mean, but when
you don't like hers, you're just
a good judge of character.

Refuse
to be controlled

Faithfulness is repeatedly, as often as you have to, denying to be controlled by things outside of your control. It is impossible to remain faithful to your calling if you think that things outside your control are inherently evil. If you concentrate on the evil in things or people, you will create the habit of blaming circumstances and others for your problems rather than believing that God works all things together for your good (see Romans 8:28). You will allow those things outside your control to in effect control you.

dive

Think about your favorite movie or book. Think about how things seemed hopeless for the hero or heroine but how in the end it all came together for their good. Life is like this; we just need to allow ourselves to see the bigger picture. What seems like hell right now might just be a setup for a life of heavenly bliss.

Selah

stop   breathe   think

Practice indifference to circumstance

God offers you freedom.
And part of that freedom
is found in letting go of those
things that you can't control, like
other people, circumstances, and
events. You can't be filled with joy and
the love of God if you are constantly filled
with fear and ambition.
Do you want to be more than a conqueror?
Then don't enter into battles with what you have
no control over. Instead pray and let God fight those
fights for you. Your freedom is found in three areas:
your will, your interpretation of events, and your use
of your thoughts.

Your joy in life is always independent from your
circumstances. Faithfully determine to be indifferent
to your circumstances *and* the Mean Girl and instead
be like the apostle Paul, who learned to be content
whatever the circumstances (Philippians 4:11).
The only way to do that is to determine to live
by that which you *can* control: your thoughts,
your prayers, your actions, and your will.
And then know that all those things *outside*
of your control are not yours to manage.
Trust that what God allows to happen
to you and around you is within his
divine will.

dive

1. Make a list of the things you can control. Be honest! If you can't control them, don't write them on the control list.

2. Now make a list of things that you can't control but wish you could (i.e., people, events, weather).

3. Look at those lists and cross out everything on the second one, all the things you can't control. Each time one of those things begins to bother you or hurt you, tell yourself, "I can't control that, so I won't fight it." You will be free when you truly realize the things you can't control and let go of trying to control them.

Have you noticed?

When she has an amazing outfit on,
she is showing off, but when you do,
you are just fashionable.

Selah

stop   breathe   think

Fear is the fuel of faith

The truly victorious soul is the one who has learned to conquer self. You have power only when you do what you don't want to do and think what other women wouldn't dare to think. Your biggest loss is when you give in to the whims of fear, emotion, and worry. But your biggest win is when you refuse to let feelings rule your life. You gain ground in the battle for peace in life if you practice self-denial, and by that I mean standing in the face of your negative feelings like fear and saying, "No, I'm not going to hide from life to protect you."

The spiritual woman doesn't demand peace of herself, but she stands in the face of trials and tribulation and refuses to be moved by them. The pain might sting and the fear might scream, but she will not be moved because she responds only to the Spirit and not to the flesh.

Remember what God said: "Be still, and know that I am God" (Psalm 46:10).

dive

1. What feelings control you most? What are the top three things that you feel the most overwhelmed by? Fear, worry, anger, loneliness? When you let emotions control your decisions and your actions, you lose peace. Decide today which emotions you will choose not to obey. Then the next time you feel them, remind yourself that they are only feelings, not fact, and turn to God for truth.

2. Oswald Chambers put it best when he said, "My goal is God Himself, not joy nor peace, nor even blessing, but Himself, my God." People who struggle for peace don't often find it, but people who give up and allow those things they can't control to happen unwittingly find themselves in that same peace they thought they had to clamor for. I find that when my goal is God himself, rather than the peace I crave, God's presence soothes my soul and I have all I ever needed.

Selah

Have you noticed?
When the boss is impressed with her,
she's a brownnoser, but when he's
smothering you with accolades,
you're a good worker.

stop   breathe   think

The *spiritual mind* has learned to think on the divine in times of trial rather than upon the trial itself

A spiritual mind has learned to think about the divine in times of trial rather than on the trial itself. With the first impulse of anger or rage, the spiritual mind removes itself from the situation and looks upon the divine, the author and perfecter of our faith. The Mean Girl in your life can be used by God to see if you will remove your eyes from him. The disciplined soul teaches itself, by doing it over and over again, to return its eyes heavenward even though every temptation is to the opposite direction. In this continual denial of our own mean urges, the spirit is perfected and grown more into the likeness of the divine.

dive

1. As John Eldredge says, you are part of an epic, part of a story so much bigger than you've ever dreamt or imagined. Think about some of your favorite movies, ones like *Titanic, Braveheart, The Lord of the Rings,* and *Gladiator,* and notice the epic nature of the stories. The reason we love these stories is because they resemble ours. The trials they must face are epic, dangerous, treacherous. But we can see the big picture, so we understand that they must pass through the trials and the testing to bring the epic to completion. Try to think of your life like an epic movie: each trial, each mess thrown at you by the Mean Girl is merely another scene that you must bravely travel through in order to get to the prize, the goal of your life.

2. Watch your favorite drama or adventure movie this week and take note of all the trials the hero must go through to save the day. If he refused the test or cowered in the corner, would the movie be as good? Think about your life and how it compares in trauma. Do you want to survive? Do you want to fight the good fight? Then remember that the spiritual soul looks heavenward—not to the cause of the pain but up to the author of our perfection.

3. When the world throws you a punch, remind yourself, as the apostle Paul reminds us, that you can be "beaten, yet not killed; sorrowful, yet always rejoicing" (2 Corinthians 6:9–10).

Have you noticed?
When she spends a lot,
she's an arrogant snob,
but when you do, you're just
investing in the economy.

Selah

stop   breathe   think

Ignore the unimportant

Spiritual perfection requires that you seek only what is important and ignore everything else. Being ignorant of things that don't concern you is actually good, because those things aren't your purpose. The pursuit of trivial things like what your Mean Girl thinks or says about you is a distraction from your purpose. Concentrate on faith and those things God asks of you. Trying to change a Mean Girl only distracts you from your purpose. Stay focused, and check yourself when you start to get important in the eyes of others. Pride can sneak up on you if you aren't continually keeping your motives and focus in check.

dive

Make a list of the important things in your life. What is your focus today? What do you have to do that can't be manipulated or controlled by the Mean Girl? Make this a list that matters: love, hope, peace. Concentrate on what you want and what God wants for you, not on the distractions she might throw your way.

Selah

The Lord doesn't allow unthankful
people to have peace.

—Athanasius

God allows everything

Most of us don't consider that both good and bad things pass through the hands of God. If you realize that both help and harm come to you only if God allows them to, then you stop blaming people and situations. Each thing, whether good or bad, is there because he has allowed it, and he will use it for your good if you will look toward him and not toward the earthly thing that brought it. When you do this, you no longer need the approval of others, and their lies and vicious gossip have little to no effect on you.

dive

1. If both bad and good truly are allowed by God, then should we not thank him for both the bad and the good? Today take five minutes to thank God for your trials and the mean women in your life and to ask him what glory he would want you to see out of this.

2. Make a list of the Mean Girls in your life, and every morning for the next week pray for them. As you do, thank God that he has given you the ability to love the way he does and to care more for others than for yourself.

Selah

stop   breathe   think

Only the unspiritual are offended

An unspiritual person is offended when difficulty and trial come her way. She is not strong because of her faith, so when her world begins to crumble, she has no refuge. But the spiritual woman who rests on truth finds peace even in the heaviest of persecution. Her eyes are no longer on the temporal but raised up toward the unseen, and she is unshakable, for she knows that the only true sin isn't against her but against God. What others have to do or say to her is of no concern, for she lives only to serve a living God, not her reputation or image. When we can let go of positioning ourselves and being concerned about what others do or say to us, we are free from the grip of manipulation and mean.

1. Mean Girls from the past often haunt us. Thoughts of them can make us cringe, even today. We dread ever seeing them again. But in order to be free from that pain, we have to let go of our right to feel hurt or offended. As believers we are called to a life of humility: "Humble yourselves before the Lord, and he will lift you up" (James 4:10). If you want to be lifted up out of the pain of a Mean Girl memory, then you must seek humility. And humility, according to *Harper's Bible Dictionary*, is "a socially acknowledged claim to neutrality in the competition of life." It is a relinquishment of the need to fit in, to be accepted, to be loved—all the things we think we "need." The key to freedom from the debilitating and painful memories is to set them free. For as Jeremy Taylor said, "Humility consists in a realistic opinion of yourself, namely, that you are an unworthy person." If we can consider ourselves unworthy, then we should not be shocked when others feel the same way about us. In fact, if we are shocked, then we are hypocrites.

2. Bible study—find a concordance or Bible study software and look up all the instances of humility and meekness. How will you practice humility with regards to other women? Have you been meek in the past? If so, what was the outcome? What do you think God had in mind when he asked us to be meek and humble?

Selah

stop   breathe   think

Don't let your defeat become your destruction

It's very easy to let the
enemy take your defeat
and turn it into destruc-
tion—but defeat ought to be a
blessing, not destruction. For time
and again Scripture tells us that we
are blessed when we are the bottom
of the rung; we are blessed when we are
persecuted and thought poorly of (see Matthew 5). Satan would steal this victory found
in our defeat and turn it against us when it should
be cause for rejoicing. Defeat should be not the end
of you but the beginning of your reliance upon God
and your faith in his ability to deliver you. This is cause
for rejoicing, for only those who truly need God ever get
to experience him.

1. In what ways have you been defeated in the world's eyes? How could God use that defeat to bless you? In what ways can you react to and learn from this defeat so that you will become a more holy and peaceful person? Use the defeat as a step to reach closer to heaven. Don't let the enemy take that from you.

2. Does a family member, a sister, a mom, or a mother-in-law try to hold your weaknesses and failures against you? These can be the hardest mean girls of all to shake—after all, they never go away. But ask yourself, what does God want *you* to learn through all of this? Take the focus off of her and put it back onto him. Search his Word for the answer. What does this thorn in your flesh prove to you about *his* strength in your weakness (see 2 Corinthians 12:7–10)?

Selah

stop   breathe   think

Exercise
thought control

Thought control is an integral part of your faith, for faith isn't based on feelings but on your will. Faith shouldn't change as your emotions do. It should be strong and determined, relentless in the face of adversity, fear, or bad memories. And your faith can only do that if you can control the wanderings of your mind, for faith has to do with believing, and belief takes place in the mind, not the emotions. Don't allow your mind to take you to places of fear and resentment. Don't let your mind wallow in grief or rejection. Your mind must find its rest in faith. It must seek the higher ground that is the home of truth. Emotions don't respond to truth any more than a crying baby responds to a reprimand. But your *mind* must respond to truth and deliberately choose it over anything you might feel. Thought control is essential to a life of faith; without it your faith will grow weak and weary, and in the end your emotions will manipulate it into something other than faith.

dive

1. Today decide to live by your will, not your emotions. If a Mean Girl from the past or present is haunting you, then change your mind. Change what you think about and how you think about things. If you can look at the things that happen to you as allowed by God, then you can begin to find the divine will in everything. Why has he allowed her? Perhaps to test you. Perhaps to prove you have faith. Perhaps because he wants you to love her. Find out why, and then do something about it.

2. Make a list of the ways you have grown or have the opportunity to grow at the hands of your Mean Girl. Search God's Word to learn about suffering, trials, and perseverance, and thank him for the opportunity to prove him faithful. Remember, in the needing is when we draw closest to our God.

Selah

stop   breathe   think

Forgive
over and over
again

People are trying to do the best they can.

When someone hurts you, mistreats you, or even acts in an evil way toward you, stop and think to yourself, *If I were her and in her place, I probably would have done the same thing. I don't know her history and her emotions, so I can't judge her actions toward me.* We don't know what God is doing in the people who hurt us. Time and again he uses these scenarios for our good, but when we won't forgive or let it go, we lose the power he is offering us.

When people don't do what you want them to do to you, exercise the gift of forgiveness and say, "Your will be done, Father." Then let it go. Don't start to look at yourself in light of her comments or evil actions or to compare yourself to the perfection you are looking for in yourself. Growing more like Christ is gradual. You fall, you get back up; you fall, you get back up.

When you forgive others over and over again, you begin to experience the peace of God. And peace is this: "You keep him in perfect peace whose mind is stayed on you, because he trusts in you" (Isaiah 26:3 ESV).

dive

1. Forgiveness doesn't mean forgetting; it just means moving on and choosing not to hold a grudge. When you refuse to love someone because of something they did, you refuse to forgive them. And unforgiveness will eventually eat you alive. Make a list of the people you haven't forgiven and decide today to forgive them. Tell God that you are sorry and that you are forgiving them. If you need to, spend some time with them, and if they are aware that you are holding a grudge, set them free by telling them you are over it.

2. How many times are you willing to forgive her? Consider the teachings of Jesus Christ, who told the men who followed him, *"and if he sins against you seven times **in the day**, and turns to you seven times, saying, 'I repent,' you must forgive him"* (Luke 17:4 ESV). Can you imagine forgiving someone seven times in one day? If I stepped on your foot six times and each time I said I was sorry, how would you react to the seventh time? Are you willing to forgive women who hurt you or who don't even know that they've hurt you? The key is to get over it. Not everything is an insult or an evil act. So don't take yourself too seriously. If they haven't committed a sin, then maybe you just need to move on and forget about it.

Selah

Have you noticed?
When she takes a lot of time
to do something, she gets
on your nerves, but when you do,
you are just being careful.

stop   breathe   think

The way to *peace* is *acceptance*

The way to peace is acceptance. Accept the things that happen to you as allowed by God. This does not mean you have to resign yourself to a miserable existence, but it does mean not getting angry when things don't go your way. Things go as things go. Accept them and move on. You can experience no forward motion without first accepting what has happened and then moving beyond it to a place free from your attachments. Don't get angry when you don't get your way. Know that events are as they are and the only thing in your control is *how you choose to remember them*. Will they be remembered as the things that destroyed you, or the things that made you holy? A soul set free knows that "God causes everything to work together for the good of those who love God and are called according to his purpose for them" (Romans 8:28 NLT).

dive

1. Have you accepted the things have happened in your life? Or do you fight against them? Do you hate them? Even hate your life? If you want peace—true, undying peace—then practice accepting the things that you cannot control, including your husband, your mother, and the Mean Girl. Trust that God knows what he is doing, and through that find inner peace.

2. If you have been holding a grudge against someone who controlled or controls your life—a coworker, a boss, a schoolmate—release that grudge today. They have control over you simply because God allows them to have control. As soon as you let go of trying to manipulate those who ultimately have the final say, the sooner you will be free to just be.

Selah

stop   breathe   think

Look fear in the eyes

A mind set on perfection understands that
the strength of spirit must first be proven. We
can grow fat and weak both physically and mentally
without exercise. And the exercise of the spirit is suffering. It is in our suffering that the Creator looks into our hearts
and weighs our character. That character is more greatly
revealed in moments of danger than in any other time. Just
like pure gold is revealed through fire, so our true self is
revealed under stress and fear. In moments of suffering
and pain, the spiritual mind remembers that this is
not punishment but a proving ground.

dive

1. When have you suffered at the hands of your Mean Girl? Retrain your mind. Look at those memories with a different set of eyes. Look at them in light of this: "Since Jesus went through everything you're going through and more, learn to think like him. Think of your sufferings as a weaning from that old sinful habit of always expecting to get your own way" (1 Peter 4:1, *The Message* paraphrase of the Bible).

2. Just as Christ took up his cross for us, so we must take up our cross. We must suffer in order to prove ourselves and to die to self. Dying to yourself—your selfish wants and desires—will purify you and make you stronger if you are willing to embrace it as a good thing and not a bad memory.

3. Consider these words from Oswald Chambers: "The Spirit of Jesus is conscious of one thing only—a perfect oneness with the Father, and He says 'Learn of Me, for I am meek and lowly in heart.' All I do ought to be founded on a perfect oneness with Him, not on a self-willed determination to be godly. This will mean that I can be easily put upon, easily over-reached, easily ignored; but if I submit to it for His sake, I prevent Jesus Christ being persecuted."

Selah

stop   breathe   think

Live in the moment

Live in the moment, for that is where you are required to live. I've never met anyone who has successfully lived in the past or the future. You must stop reliving the pain of the past as if by reliving it you might somehow change it. The present is all you really have control of, and no amount of pondering will fix the past. Don't seek to identify your wounds or try to explain them. God never calls us to that; instead he asks us to die to self and our need to know why this or that happened to us. He calls us to humble ourselves before him, trusting that everything that has ever happened to us has been allowed to happen to us by him. He promises that he is in control and that he will make it all work out (Romans 8:28).

The pain and suffering that a Mean Girl in your past might have caused is there for blessing, not for analysis. *"Blessed is the man who perseveres under trial, because when he has stood the test, he will receive the crown of life that God has promised to those who love him"* (James 1:12). Standing the test is not seeking to answer *"Why me?"* but responding *"As you wish, Lord."*

dive

1. The past is over, and now all you have is how you think about it. What are your thoughts with regard to your Mean Girl? Are you willing to let go of the pain and to march on toward your heavenly Father? Make that decision today.

2. Think about how you have been affected by your memories of the Mean Girl. A mother once told me that she hadn't realized it, but her resentment for the girls she went to school with had tainted her relationship with her own daughters. She took out her distaste for females on her own children. Have you allowed your relationships with females to be tainted by the past? Think about the ways you have protected yourself from Mean Girls or tortured yourself with their memory. Make it your goal to erase that effect. Make it your goal to stop the insanity and to live only in the present.

3. Bible study—find at least five verses on God's sovereignty. Use these verses to remind you that he is in control, even of the past.

Selah

stop   breathe   think

the **end**
of the journey

Mean or not mean,
that is the question

Look at the following list and score yourself, with 1 describing you not at all and 10 describing you exactly:

When someone hurts me, I can forgive that person.

1 2 3 4 5 6 7 8 9 10

I don't like getting revenge.

1 2 3 4 5 6 7 8 9 10

I never gossip.

1 2 3 4 5 6 7 8 9 10

No pain, no gain.

1 2 3 4 5 6 7 8 9 10

God has a reason for everything.

1 2 3 4 5 6 7 8 9 10

Life isn't fair and that's okay.

1 2 3 4 5 6 7 8 9 10

Not everyone has to like me.

1 2 3 4 5 6 7 8 9 10

Score:

35 or higher: *Bravo, fair one.* You have done well. Your spirit is bright and so is your outlook on life, faithful one. But if you didn't get a perfect 70, you might still have some areas to work on in order to bring ultimate peace into your life. Don't put this book away; keep it as a pick-me-up, a chance to bring refreshment to your staggering soul.

21–34: *Dark one,* come into the light. Living life on the verge of a pity party or angry outburst doesn't bring you the peace that your soul longs for. Think about who you want to be and how you want to feel. If you are tired of being depressed and down a lot of the time, then maybe a more honest look inside at how you handle the mean in your life is still needed. You might want to give this book another read and let it seep into your pores a little more. It's never too late to refresh your tired spirit.

7–20: *Dear warrior,* not all of life has to be a fight. Remember, there is a bigger picture than you can see right now. All the energy you are spending in order to control your world is only spinning you out of control. You might not even realize it right now, but you are void of any peace and your spirit is withering from dryness. If you haven't read it yet, pick up a copy of *Mean Girls All Grown Up.* It might be just what you need to clear the cobwebs from your spirit.

For moral support or a virtual shoulder to lean on, check out www.meangirls.net.

Selah. Stop. Breathe. Think.

As I said at the beginning, this book is about you from front to back. Hopefully you've had time to reflect, time to ponder, and time to dream. I pray that your soul is now somehow lighter, more hopeful, and more determined. This has been an arduous journey, but one well worth the taking. Consider where you've come from and know where you are going. Take a look at the very first journal entry you made, your spiritual inventory, and now look at your life from the other side of this book. What have you learned? How have you changed? What will you do differently? Speak to your soul about life, love, and hope. Write your future. Commit to the possibilities of a deeper spiritual life.

How has the way you think about Mean Girls changed?

Selah

How could your spiritual life be better?

What three things will you commit to do in the next week
that will draw you closer in your relationship with God?

How will you act around Mean Girls in the future?

NOW LEAVING
MEANVILLE

stop   breathe   think

This exercise might seem a bit morbid, but bear with me. What I want you to do now is to think about the end of your life. How will the years you have spent on earth look to someone who lives long after you are gone? What will you have done, changed, or contributed to the world? As you think about this, you will begin to direct your steps for the future and begin to make purposeful decisions in all you do.

Now think about your funeral. All your family and friends will be there to say good-bye and remember the amazing you. Someone will give a eulogy, a testimony of your life, the things you accomplished and the people whose lives you touched. What I want you to do is to write your eulogy. In a paragraph or two, describe your life as if you were looking back over the years of a long life. What have you done? Who were you to people? How did you change lives? This exercise will set the pace for who you will become. Years ago in high school I did this same thing. I've since gone on to complete over half the things in my eulogy, including writing five books. Join me on a journey of the possible and define a life of hope and love.

Selah

NOW LEAVING
MEANVILLE

stop   breathe   think

Selah

Now the beginning of a life of understanding is yours. If you are willing to believe God's Word and trust that it will never fail you, then you are free to fly and soar on wings like eagles. The mean women in your life will never again trip you or hold you down. A spirit set on things above is free to run and not grow weary. What others think or say about you is now inconsequential in so far as they are attempting to assassinate your spirit. Give thought daily to God's call on your life, understanding and living by his Word. Focus your energy on pleasing him, and you will experience a life of change. Take heart! You have the strength! You have the courage! You have the hope! Now go and be free!

stop   breathe   think

Hayley DiMarco writes cutting-edge books including *Mean Girls All Grown Up*, *Mean Girls: Facing Your Beauty Turned Beast*, *Marriable*, the best-selling *Dateable: Are You? Are They?*, *The Dateable Rules*, and *The Dirt on Breaking Up*. Her goal is to give practical answers for life's problems and encourage girls and women to form stronger spiritual lives. From traveling the world with a French theater troupe to working for a little shoe company called Nike and then being the idea girl behind the success of the Biblezine *Revolve*, Hayley has seen a lot of life and decided to make a difference in her world. Hayley founded Hungry Planet, a think tank that feeds the world's appetite for truth through authors, speakers, and consultants. Hungry Planet helps organizations understand and reach the postmodern generation, while Hungry Planet books tackle life's everyday issues with a distinctly modern spiritual voice.

For more information on Hayley and Mean Girls, visit www.meangirls.net.

For information on Hungry Planet, log on to www.hungry planet.net.

Don't Miss Mean Girls All Grown Up!

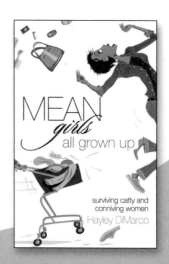